Dedication

This little book is dedicated to my amazing grandsons,

Jude Allan
Oliver Hughes

Thanks for bringing your smiles to so many of us!

About the Illustrator

Special thanks to the entire Creative Team at American Web Builders

- Nick Bateman
- Gordon Chase
- M. Daniel Baig
- H. Bintory
- Danny
- Marcus Long

Who Said I Am Amazing?

I can stand on one leg, clap my hands and sing without falling over. And if I fall, I can get right back up because I am AMAZING!

Who Said I Am Brilliant?

I like to read and learn things everyday. Because I read I can travel all over the world without even leaving my house because I am BRILLIANT!

Who Said I Am Courageous?

Sometimes I am afraid a little, but I am COURAGEOUS like a knight.

Who Said I Am Dependable?

I know when it's my bedtime I have to brush my teeth and go to bed just like I'm told because I am DEPENDABLE!

Who Said I Am Energetic?

I have so much energy. Sometimes I love to run up and down stairs and roll down hills because I am ENERGETIC!

F

Who Said I Am Funny?

I love to laugh and make my friends laugh too because I am FUNNY!

Who Said I Am Generous?

I like to share my toys and candy with my friends because I am GENEROUS!

Who said I Am Helpful?

I like to help my Mom make the beds and help my Dad rake the leaves because I am HELPFUL!

I

Who Said I Am Intelligent?

I can color beautiful pictures and write my own name because I am INTELLIGENT!

Who Said I Am Joyful?

I like to whistle when I work because it makes work fun. I whistle because I am JOYFUL!

Who Said I Am Kind?

I open the door for my Mom when she's carrying groceries because I am KIND!

Who Said I Am Loved?

My Mom and Dad love me. My Grandparents love me too. My friends love me. My teacher loves me. I am LOVED!

Who Said I Am Magnificent?

After my bath I get dressed and look in the mirror and see myself. I am MAGNIFICENT!

Who Said I Am Neat?

I like to put my toys away and brush my hair because I am NEAT!

Who Said I Am Obedient?

I understand the difference between what is right and what is wrong. I like to do the right thing all the time because I am OBEDIENT!

Who said I Am Patriotic?

I love to pledge allegiance to our flag and pray for our country because I am PATRIOTIC!

"And to the Republic for which it stands, one nation under God…"

 **Who Said I Am Quiet?**

I never talk out loud in church. I pray using my soft voice. Sometimes I am very QUIET!

S Who Said I Am Strong?

I use my muscles when I do my chores at home because I am STRONG!

T Who Said I Am **T**rustworthy?

My friends can trust me with secrets because I am TRUSTWORTHY!

U

Who Said I Am Unique?

There is only one me! I am UNIQUE!

V Who Said I Am Valuable?

I am more important than all the diamonds, emeralds, and rubies in the world! I am VALUABLE!

W

Who Said I Am Wonderful?

I have so many things about me that I really like because I am WONDERFUL!

Who Said I Am eXtra Special?

I love to sing and dance. I can jump so high that I can almost touch the sky because I am EXTRA SPECIAL!

Who Said I Am Yours?

Y

When I say my prayers at night, God tells me that I belong to Him and that He belongs to me. So, every night I tell Him that I am YOURS!

Who Said I Am Zealous?

I am full of joy and like to smile.
I like to make others feel happy
because I am ZEALOUS!

Who Said I Am?

God said, "I Am". That's

who said, "I am"!

YOU are God's amazing child.

YOU are above all the angels.

YOU are made in His image.

YOU have authority over all living things on earth.

YOU are filled with God's spirit.

God sacrificed His only Son for YOU because He loves YOU so much.

YOU will never be alone because God is with YOU always, even until the end of time.

Jesus loves me this I know, For the Bible tells me so.
God doesn't make junk! He made us in HIS image, and He loves ME! I am God's highest form of creation!

Exodus 3:14 And God said to Moses, "I am who I am".

www.ingramcontent.com/pod-product-compliance
Lightning Source LLC
Chambersburg PA
CBHW060502010526
44118CB00018B/2504